The Silly Little Book of JOKES ABOUT BOYS

The Silly Little Book of

JOKES ABOUT BOYS

p

This is a Parragon Book

This edition published in 2002

Parragon
Queen Street House
4 Queen Street
Bath BA1 1HE, UK

Produced by Magpie Books an imprint of
Robinson Publishing Ltd, London

Hardback ISBN 0-75258-623-8
Paperback ISBN 0-75258-631-9

A copy of the British Library Cataloguing-in-Publication Data is available from the British Library

Printed and bound in China

Contents

BOYS WILL BE BOYS 1

EDUCATIONAL DISCORD 42

BROTHERS IN ARMS 60

LIKE A FISH NEEDS A BICYCLE 78

THAT'S MY BOY 85

HE SAID THAT DID HE? 102

WHO NEEDS ENEMIES? 128

KNOCK, KNOCK 146

GRAFFITI RULES, OK 167

RIDICULOUS RIDDLES 188

THERE ONCE WAS A BAD GUY . . . 219

GET YOUR MOUTH AROUND THESE! 234

Introduction

Whether your nickname is Fog (because you're thick and wet), you're a dizzy boy scout (spend all day doing good turns), or you're the son of Dracula (and a pain in the neck), this book is an education! So read on and have a laugh at your own expense. And girls – don't think this book isn't for you! Here is your biggest chance yet to get even with that nice boy next door . . .

Boys Will Be Boys

What happened when the wizard turned a naughty boy into a hare?
He's still rabbiting on about it.

Did you hear about the boy who wanted to run away to the circus?
He ended up in a flea circus.

1st Boy: Are you having a party for your birthday?
2nd Boy: No, I'm having a witch do.
1st Boy: What's a witch do?
2nd Boy: She flies around on a broomstick casting spells.

Wizard: What's the matter son?
Young wizard: The boy next door says I look just like you?
Wizard: What did you say?
Young wizard: Nothing, he's bigger than me.

Did you hear about the boy who saw a witch riding on a broomstick?
He said, "What are you doing on that?"
She replied, "My sister's got the vacuum cleaner."

How do you know you are haunted by a parrot?
He keeps saying, "Oooo's a pretty boy then?"

Why did the stupid boy wear a turtle neck sweater?
To hide his flea collar.

Why did the boy take an aspirin after hearing a werewolf howl?
Because it gave him an eerie ache.

A little boy came running into the kitchen. "Dad, dad," he said, "there's a monster at the door with a really ugly face."
"Tell him you've already got one," said his father.

Why was the boy unhappy to win the prize for the best costume at the Halloween party?
Because he just came to pick up his little sister.

One day a boy was walking down the street when he saw a sea monster standing on the corner looking lost. The boy put a leash on the sea monster and took him to the police station.

"You should take him to the museum," said the policeman.

The next day the policeman saw the boy in the town again with the monster on a leash. "I thought I told you to take him to the museum," said the policeman.

"I did," said the boy, "and today I'm taking him to the cinema."

A boy went to a Halloween party with a sheet over his head. "Are you here as a ghost?" asked his friends.

"No, I'm an unmade bed."

Another boy wore a sheet over his head. "Are you an unmade bed?" asked his friends.

"No, I'm an undercover agent," he replied.

Why did the boy carry a clock and a bird on Halloween?
It was for "tick or tweet."

That boy is so dirty, the only time he washes his ears is when he eats watermelon.

Did you hear about the dizzy Boy Scout?
He spent all day doing good turns.

A boy went into a cafe and ordered a can of cola. He took a can opener from his pocket, opened the can and drank the cola. The girl behind the counter asked why he didn't use the ring pull to open the can and he replied, "Oh, I thought that was only for people that didn't have a can opener with them."

George is the type of boy that his mother doesn't want him to associate with!

Boy Monster: You've got a face like a million dollars.
Girl Monster: Have I really?
Boy Monster: Yes – it's green and wrinkly.

What's the difference between a crossword expert, a greedy boy and a pot of glue?
A crossword expert is a good puzzler and the greedy boy's a pud guzzler.
The pot of glue? Oh, that's where you get stuck!

A little boy came downstairs crying late one night. "What's wrong?" asked his mother.

"Do people really come from dust, like they said in church?" he sobbed.

"In a way they do," said his mother.

"And when they die do they turn back to dust?"

"Yes, they do."

The little boy began to cry again.

"Well, under my bed there's someone either coming or going."

What do you get if you cross a zombie with a Boy Scout?
A creature that scares old ladies across the road.

How did the invisible boy upset his mother?
He kept appearing.

Igor: How was that science fiction movie you saw last night?
Dr Frankenstein: Oh, the same old story – boy meets girl, boy loses girl, boy builds new girl . . .

Did you hear about the boy who got worried when his nose grew to be eleven inches long?
He thought it might turn into a foot.

A man out for a walk came across a little boy pulling his cat's tail.
"Hey, you!" he shouted, "don't pull the cat's tail!"
"I'm not pulling!" replied the little boy. "I'm only holding on – the cat's pulling!"

There was a little boy who had really smelly feet. One night before he went to bed his mother told him that tomorrow was a very special day and that when he woke up his feet wouldn't smell at all. The boy was so excited he hardly slept. But, eventually, he dropped off. Next morning, his mother woke him early. The first thing he did was to sniff his feet. They smelled even worse than before. His mother just laughed and said, "April Fool!"

A farmer was showing a schoolboy round his farm when they came to a field where the farmer's sheep were grazing. "How many sheep do you reckon there are?" the farmer asked proudly.

"Seven hundred and sixty-four," replied the boy after a few seconds.

The farmer gasped. "That's exactly right, boy. How did you count them so quickly?"

"Simple," said the boy genius, "I just counted the legs and divided by four!"

Did you hear about the doctor who crossed a parrot with a vampire? It bit his neck, sucked his blood, and said, "Who's a pretty boy then?"

Did you hear about the little boy who was named after his father? They called him Dad.

Cannibal: Mom, mom, I've been eating a missionary and I feel sick.
Mom: Well, you know what they say – you can't keep a good man down.

An old lady saw a little boy with a fishing rod over his shoulder and a jar of tadpoles in his hand walking through the park one Sunday.

"Little boy," she called, "don't you know you shouldn't go fishing on a Sunday?"

"I'm not going fishing missus," he called back, "I'm going home."

Did you hear about the two little boys who found themselves in a modern art gallery by mistake?

"Quick," said one, "run! Before they say we did it!"

A little boy went into a baker's.
"How much are those cakes?" he asked.
"Two for 25 cents," said the baker.
"How much does one cost?" asked the boy.
"13 cents," said the baker.
"Then I'll take the other one for 12 cents!" said the boy.

"Doc, I just wanted to let you know that there is an invisible man in your waiting room."
"Tell him I can't see him now. Next!"

A boy had the bad luck to break a leg playing soccer. After his leg had been put in a cast, he asked the doctor, "When you take the plaster off, will I be able to play the violin?"

"Of course you will," said the doctor reassuringly.

"That's funny," said the boy, "I've never been able to play it before."

Roy: They say ignorance is bliss.

Rita: Then you should be the happiest boy in the world.

"My boyfriend says I look like a dishy Italian!" said Miss Conceited.

"He's right," said her little brother. "Sophia Loren?"

"No – spaghetti!"

"Keep that dog out of my garden. It smells disgusting!" a neighbor said to a small boy one day. The boy went home to tell everyone to stay away from the neighbor's garden because of the smell!

Did you hear about the boy who sat under a cow?
He got a pat on the head.

Did you hear about the boy who was known as Fog?
He was dense and wet.

Sid: Mom, all the boys at school call me Big Head.
Mom: Never mind, dear, just run down to the grocery store for me and collect the 5 pounds of potatoes I ordered in your cap.

Good news: two boys went out one day climbing trees.
Bad news: one of them fell out.
Good news: there was a hammock beneath him.
Bad news: there was a rake beside the hammock.
Good news: he missed the rake.
Bad news: he missed the hammock, too.

What happened to the boy who turned into an insect?
He beetled off.

As two boys were passing the rectory, the minister leaned over the wall and showed them a ball.

"Is this yours?" he asked.

"Did it do any damage?" asked one of the boys.

"No," replied the minister.

"Then it's mine."

Did you hear about the boy who stole some rhubarb?

He was put into custardy.

Two boys camping out in a backyard wanted to know the time, so they began singing at the top of their voices. Eventually a neighbor threw open his window and shouted down at them, "Hey! Less noise! Don't you know what the time is? It's three o'clock!"

A monster goes to a gas station and says: Fill me up.
The gas man replies: You have to have a car for me to do that!
The monster replies to the gas man: But I had a car for lunch!

A witch went into a candy store to buy some sweets. The boy behind the counter said, "Gosh, you are really ugly aren't you? I've never seen anyone as offensively hideous as you."

"Young man," she replied, "I didn't come in here to be insulted."

"Really?" he said. "Where do you usually go?"

A boy in a movie theater notices what looks like a bear sitting next to him. "Are you a bear?"

"Yes."

"What are you doing at the movies?"

"Well, I liked the book."

A boy was staying in a big old country house, and in the middle of the night he met a ghost. The ghost said, "I have been walking these corridors for 300 years."

The boy said, "In that case, can you tell me the way to the bathroom?"

Three boys are walking along the beach one day when they see a cave. The first boy goes in and is just looking at a banknote on a big rock when a ghostly voice calls out, "I am the ghost of Auntie Mabel and this five dollars stays on the table!"

The second boy goes in and is reaching for the money when the same thing happens again.

The third boy goes in, sees the five dollars and cries out, "I am the ghost of David Crockett and this five dollars goes in my pocket!"

"You can have that brain there for $3,000," said the brain surgeon to the boy who was going to have a brain transplant. "It used to belong to a bank manager. This one's $1,000: it was a dancer's. And this one's $50,000: it belonged to a school teacher."

"Why's it ten times more than the others?" gasped the boy.

"It's been used ten times less than theirs!"

A boy telephoned O'Hare Airport.
"How long does it take to get to New York?"
"Just a minute."
"Thanks very much."

A garbage man was walking along whistling while balancing a bin on his head and one on each shoulder.
"How do you manage to do that?" asked Jack.
"It's easy," replied the dustman, "Just put your lips together and blow."

A man sat playing chess with a huge, hairy, purple monster in a pub. A stranger came in and sat down and in amazement watched them playing. When they had finished the game he came over. "I'm a movie producer," he explained as he introduced himself. "Your monster could make a fortune in Hollywood." The man just shrugged. "He's not that clever," he said dismissively, "I've just beaten him three times in the last four games."

A boy went into the local department store where he saw a sign on the escalator – "Dogs must be carried on this escalator." The boy then spent the next two hours looking for a dog.

Two boys went into a very dark, spooky cave. "I can't see a thing," said one.

"Hold my hand," said the other.

"OK." The first boy reached out.

"Take off that horrible bristly glove first, though."

"But I'm not wearing a glove . . ."

1st Ghoulish Fiend: I had a nice man to dinner last night.

2nd Ghoulish Fiend: So you enjoyed having him?

1st Ghoulish Fiend: Oh, yes, he was delicious.

A boy at a swimming pool climbed up to the high diving board. He paused, lifted his arms, and was about to dive when the attendant came running up, shouting, "Don't dive – there's no water in that pool!"
"That's OK," said the boy. "I can't swim!"

"Dad, there's a man at the door collecting for the new swimming pool."
"Give him a glass of water!"

"You boy!" called a policeman. "Can you help? We're looking for a man with a huge red nose called Cotters . . ."
"Really?" said the boy. "What're his ears called?"

"May I have some two-handed cheese, please?" a boy in a restaurant asked the waiter.
"What do you mean 'two-handed cheese'?" asked the waiter.
"Yes, the kind you eat with one hand and hold your nose with the other."

"What's your new perfume called?" a young man asked his girlfriend.
"'High Heaven'", she replied.
"I asked what it was called, not what it smells to!"

A boy with a newt on his shoulder walked into a library. "What do you call him?" asked the librarian.
"Tiny", said the boy.
"Why do you call him 'Tiny'?"
"Because he's my newt!"

Insect Films: The Fly; Batman; Beetlejuice; The Sting; The Good, the Bug and the Ugly; Spawn; The Frog Prince; Four Webbings and a Funeral; Seven Bats for Seven Brothers.

An American tourist was visiting a quaint country village, and got talking to an old man in the local pub. "And have you lived here all your life, sir?" asked the American.
"Not yet, m'dear," said the villager wisely.

A boy sat on a train chewing gum and staring vacantly into space, when suddenly an old woman sitting opposite said, "It's no good you talking to me, young man, I'm stone deaf!"

Why did the boy take a pencil to bed?
To draw the curtains . . . I'd tell you another joke about a pencil, but it doesn't have a point.

Have you ever seen a man-eating tiger?
No, but in the restaurant next door I once saw a man eating chicken!

Happily innocent of all golfing lore, young Sam watched with interest the efforts of the man in the bunker to play his shot. At last, the ball rose amid a cloud of sand, hovered in the air, and then dropped on the green and rolled into the hole. "Oh my," Sam chuckled, "he'll have a tough time getting out of that one!"

Why did the lazy boy get a job in a bakery?
Because he wanted a good loaf.

A naughty child was irritating all the passengers on the flight from London to New York. At last one man could stand it no longer. "Hey kid," he shouted, "why don't you go outside and play?"

What's the difference between a boy and E.T.?
E.T. phoned home.

A man coughed violently, and his false teeth shot across the room and smashed against the wall.

"Oh dear," he wailed, "whatever shall I do? I can't afford a new set."

"Don't worry," said a little boy, "I'll get a pair from my Dad for you."

The next day the boy came back with the teeth, which fitted perfectly.

"This is wonderful," said the man. "Your father must be a very good dentist."

"Oh, he's not a dentist," replied the boy, "he's an undertaker."

A boy is in a prison cell with no windows and no doors; there are no holes in the ceiling or trapdoors in the floor, yet in the morning the jailers find him gone. How did he get out?

Through the doorway – there were no doors remember!

Educational Discord

On her holidays, the geography teacher explained to the history teacher that she went to the Himalayas, visiting remote mountain areas. "In fact," she said, "we went where the hand of man has never set foot."

"Why is your name the same as the principal's?" a new boy at school asked his teacher.

"Because he's my father!"

"Did you know that when you took the job?"

"I see you've got that new boy down for the football game against Township High," said the English teacher to the coach.
"Yes, but I'm not sure what position to play him."
"Well, if his football's anything like his English, he's a natural drawback."

Teacher: That's the stupidest boy in the whole school.
Mother: That's my son.
Teacher: Oh! I'm so sorry.
Mother: You're sorry?

A little boy ran home from school on the first day and pestered his mother into taking him into a toy shop. When they got there he insisted that she buy him a gun.
"But why do you need a gun?" asked his mother.
"Because our teacher told us she was going to teach us to draw tomorrow."

When George left school he was going to be a printer. All the teachers said he was the right type.

"We're going to play elephants and circuses," said a little boy at kindergarten, "do you want to join in?"

"I'd love to," replied the teacher. "What do you want me to do?"

"You can be the lady that feeds us peanuts!"

A little boy came home from his first day at kindergarten and said to his mother, "What's the use of going to school? I can't read, I can't write, and the teacher won't let me talk."

Rich boy to dinner lady: This bread's horrible! Why can't you make your own bread like the servants do at home?
Dinner lady: Because we don't have the kind of dough that your father makes!

Did you hear about the boy who had to do a project on trains? He had to keep track of everything!

"Why don't you like this country?" the teacher asked a Californian boy who had come to an English school.

"It's the weather," drawled Bud. "I'm not used to the rain. At home we have 365 days of sunshine every year – at least."

"What were you before you came to school, boys and girls?" asked the teacher, hoping that someone would say "babies." She was disappointed when all the children cried out, "Happy!"

The teacher was furious with her son. "Just because you've been put in my class, there's no need to think you can take liberties. You're a pig!"

The boy said nothing.

"Well! Do you know what a pig is?"

"Yes, Mom," said the boy, "the offspring of a swine."

Miss Smith says that I've got such bad handwriting that I ought to be a doctor!

"I'd like you to be very quiet today, boys and girls. I've got a dreadful headache."

"Excuse me," said Alec, "why don't you do what Mom does when she has a headache?"

"What's that?"

"She sends us out to play."

"I hope you're not one of those boys who sits and watches the school clock," said the principal to a new boy.

"No, Sir. I've got a digital watch that bleeps at three-fifteen."

The principal was very proud of his school's academic record. "It is very impressive," said one parent who was considering sending his son there. "How do you maintain such high standards?"

"Simple," said the principal. "The school motto says it all."

"What's that?" asked the parent.

"If at first you don't suceed, you're expelled."

Ben's teacher regards Ben as a wonder child. He wonders whether he'll ever learn anything.

"How old would you say I am, Francis?" the teacher asked.

"Forty," said the boy promptly.

"You seem very sure," said the puzzled teacher. "What makes you think I'm 40?"

"My big brother's 20," replied the boy, "and you're twice as silly as he is!"

Teacher: Why couldn't your brother spell "Mississippi" when I asked him this afternoon in class?

Boy: Because he didn't know if you meant the river or the state!

Was the principal's brother really a missionary?
He certainly was. He gave the people of the Cannibal Islands their first taste of Christianity.

An English teacher asked her class to write an essay on what they'd do if they had a million dollars. Alec handed in a blank sheet of paper. "Alec!" yelled the teacher, "you've done nothing. Why?"
"Cuz if I had a million dollars, that's exactly what I would do."

"I'm not going to school today," Alexander said to his mother. "The teachers bully me, and the boys in my class don't like me."

"You're going. And that's final. I'll give you two good reasons why."

"Why?"

"Firstly, you're 35 years old. Secondly, you're the principal."

"Now remember boys and girls," said the science teacher. "You can tell a tree's age by counting the rings in a cross section. One ring for each year."
Alec went home for dinner and found they were having a jelly roll for dessert. "I'm not eating that, Mom," he said, "it's five years old!"

I enjoy doing my homework
Even at weekends,
But my best friend's just told me
He thinks I'm round the bend.

Teacher: Who was that on the phone, Sammy?
Sammy: No one important, Miss Smith. Just some man who said it was long distance from Australia, so I told him I knew that already.

A hillbilly dragged his protesting son to a new school which had just opened in a nearby village. When they arrived, he took his son to see the teacher. "Howdy," said the hillbilly. "This here's my son, Arthur. Now what kind of learnin' are you teachin'?"

"Oh, all the usual subjects," said the teacher, nodding at the boy. "Reading, writing, arithmetic."

"What's this?" interrupted the father. "Arith... arith... What did you say?"

"Arithmetic, sir," said the teacher, "instruction in geometry, algebra, and trigonometry."

"Trigonometry!" cried the delighted hillbilly. "That's what my boy needs. He's the worst darn shot in the family."

The school teacher was furious when Alec knocked him down with his new bicycle in the playground. "Don't you know how to ride that yet?" he roared.

"Sure!" shouted Alec over his shoulder. "It's the bell I can't work yet."

Simple Simon was writing a geography essay. It began like this: The people who live in Paris are called parasites . . .

"Hello, Billy. Do you like your new school?" asked Uncle Ned.

"Sometimes," said the boy.

"When is that?"

"When it's closed."

First Teacher: What's wrong with young Jimmy today? I saw him running round the playground screaming and pulling at his hair!

Second Teacher: Don't worry. He's just lost his marbles.

Brothers in Arms

Little brother: Look bro, I've got a pack of cards.
Big brother: Big deal!

Mommy monster: What are you doing with that saw and where's your little brother?
Young monster: Hee, hee! He's my half-brother now.

Did the bionic monster have a brother?
No, but he had lots of trans-sisters.

A small boy walked into a police station one day and said, "I've got three big brothers and we all live in the same room. My eldest brother has seven cats. Another one has three dogs, and the third has a goat. I want you to do something about the smell."
"Are there windows in your room?" asked the officer.
"Yes, of course there are!" said the boy.
"Have you tried opening them?"
"What, and lose all my pigeons?"

"What's your father's occupation?" asked the school secretary on the first day of the new academic year.

"He's a conjurer, Ma'am," said the new boy.

"How interesting. What's his favorite trick?"

"He saws people in half."

"Gosh! Now, next question. Any brothers and sisters?"

"One half brother and two half sisters."

A small ghost was sitting in a haunted house all alone when another ghost came in. It said, "Hello, I'm your long lost brother." The first ghost replied, "Oooo?"

My big brother is such an idiot. The other day I saw him hitting himself on the head with a hammer. He was trying to make his head swell so his hat wouldn't fall over his eyes.

Did you hear about the little spook who couldn't sleep at night because his brother kept telling him human stories?

A little monster was learning to play the violin. "I'm good, aren't I?" he asked his big brother.
"You should be on the radio," said his brother.
"You think I'm that good?"
"No, I think you're terrible, but if you were on the radio, I could switch you off.

"Charley, why did Farley run through the screen door?" asked Mom.

"Because he wanted to strain himself."

Dad: Don't be selfish. Let your brother use the sled half the time.

Son: I do, Dad. I use it going down the hill, and he gets to use it coming up.

Ned: Boy! Was I ever in hot water last night!
Ed: You were? What did you do?
Ned: I took a bath.

Why did your brother go to night school?
Because he wanted to learn to read in the dark.

Did you hear about my brother? He saw a moose's head hanging on a wall and went into the next room to see the rest of it.

Charley wanted to buy Farley a birthday cake, but he couldn't figure out how to get the cake in the typewriter so he could type "Happy birthday."

Mom: Why does your little brother jump up and down before taking his medicine?

Boy: Because he read the label, and it said "shake well before using."

My brother's been practicing the violin for ten years.
Is he any good?
No. It was nine years before he found out he wasn't supposed to blow.

Mom: What are you doing son?
Boy: Writing my brother a letter.
Mom: That's a lovely idea, dear, but why are you writing so slowly?
Boy: Because he can't read very fast.

Little brother: If you broke your arm in two places, what would you do?
Big brother: I wouldn't go back to those two place, that's for sure.

My brother's just opened a shop.
Really? How's he doing?
Six months. He opened it with a crowbar.

Big brother: That planet over there is Mars.
Little brother: Then that other one must be Pa's.

My brother's one of the biggest stickup men in town.
Gosh, is he really?
Yes, he's a six-foot-six billposter.

Why did your brother ask your father to sit in the freezer?
Because she wanted an ice-cold pop.

Little brother: I'm going to buy a sea horse.
Big brother: Why?
Little brother: Because I want to play water polo.

Why does your brother wear a life jacket in bed?

Because he sleeps on a waterbed!

My brother's a professional boxer.

Heavyweight?

No, featherweight. He tickles his opponents to death.

My dad once stopped a man ill-treating a donkey. It was a case of brotherly love.

So you are distantly related to the family next door, are you?
Yes – their dog is our dog's brother.

A scoutmaster asked one of his troop what good deed he had done for the day. "Well," said the Scout. "Mom had only one dose of castor oil left, so I let my baby brother have it."

Charlie had a puppy on a leash. He met Farley and said, "I just got this puppy for our little brother."
"Really?" said Farley. "Who in the world did you find to make a swap like that?"

First Boy: My brother said he'd tell me everything he knows.

Second Boy: He must have been speechless.

First Boy: Why is your brother always flying off the handle?

Second Boy: Because he's got a screw loose.

Peter: My brother wants to work badly.

Anita: As I remember, he usually does.

Dan: My little brother is a real pain.
Nan: Things could be worse.
Dan: How?
Nan: He could be twins.

First Boy: My brother's on a seafood diet.
Second Boy: Really?
First Boy: Yes, the more he sees food the more he eats.

First Boy: Does your brother keep himself clean?

Second Boy: Oh, yes! He takes a bath every month whether he needs one or not.

May: What position does your brother play in the school football team?

Jay: I think he's one of the drawbacks.

Like a Fish Needs a Bicycle

What did the cannibal's parents say when she brought her boyfriend home?
"Lovely, dear, he looks good enough to eat!"

Girlfriend: Shall I give that tramp one of my cakes?
Boyfriend: Why, what harm has he ever done you?

Your sister's boyfriend certainly has staying power. In fact, he never leaves.

Nan: My boyfriend really embarrassed me yesterday. We were at a very expensive restaurant and he drank his tea with his little finger sticking out.
Dan: But that's considered polite in some circles.
Nan: Not with the teabag hanging from it, it's not.

Waiter! Waiter! What's this creepy crawly thing doing on my girlfriend's shoulder?
I don't know – friendly thing isn't he?

1st Witch: What's your new boyfriend like?
2nd Witch: He's mean, nasty, ugly, smelly, and totally evil – but he has some bad points, too.

Doctor! Doctor! My boyfriend smells like a fish.
Poor sole!

My boyfriend only has two faults: everything he says and everything he does!

Girlfriend: Will you love me when I'm old and fat and ugly?
Boyfriend: Of course I do!

Handsome Harry: Every time I walk past a girl she sighs.
Wisecracking William: With relief!

Jane: Do you like me?
Wayne: As girls go, you're fine. And the sooner you go the better!

1st Cannibal: I don't know what to make of my boyfriend these days.
2nd Cannibal: How about a hotpot?

Flash Harry gave his girlfriend a mink stole for her birthday. Well, it may not have been mink, but it's fairly certain it was stole.

Freda: Boys whisper they love me.
Fred: Well, they wouldn't admit it out loud, would they?

My brother's looking for a wife. Trouble is, he can't find a woman who loves him as much as he loves himself.

When Wally Witherspoon proposed to his girlfriend she said, "I love the simple things in life, Wally, but I don't want one of them for a husband."

That's My Boy

What did the cannibal mom say to her son who was chasing a missionary?
Stop playing with your food!

What did the vampire do to stop his son biting his nails?
He cut all his fingers off.

The optician's boy is making a spectacle of himself.

What parting gift did the mommy werewolf give to her son when he left home?
A comb.

"William," shouted his Mom. "There were two pieces of cake in the pantry last night and now there's only one. How do you explain that?"
"It was dark in the pantry, Mom," explained William, "and I didn't see the other piece."

1st Monster: What is that son of yours doing these days?
2nd Monster: He's at medical school.
1st Monster: Oh, what's he studying?
2nd Monster: Nothing, they're studying him.

Son: Dad, the dentist wasn't painless like he said he would be.
Dad: Did he hurt you, then?
Son: No, but he did yell when I bit his finger!

Mom: Haven't you finished filling the salt shaker yet?
Son: Not yet. It's really hard to get the salt through all those little holes.

Little Johnny was crying one day, and his dad asked him why. "I've lost five cents," sobbed Johnny.
"Don't worry," said his dad kindly. "Here's five more for you."
At this, Johnny howled louder than ever. "Now what is it?" asked his dad.
"I wish I'd said I'd lost ten cents!"

1st Witch: I took my son to the zoo yesterday.
2nd Witch: Really, did they keep him?

"I want you to help me stop my son gambling," an anxious father said to his boy's principal. "I don't know where he gets it from, but it's bet, bet, bet."
"Leave it to me," said the principal.
A week later he phoned the boy's father. "I think I've cured him," he said.
"How?"

"Well, I saw him looking at my beard and he said, 'I bet that's a false beard.' How much? I said, and he said '$5'."

"What happened?" asked the father.

"Well he tugged my beard which is quite natural, and I made him give me $5. I'm sure that'll teach him a lesson."

"No, it won't," said the father. "He bet me $10 on Monday that he'd pull your beard with your permission by the end of the week!"

"Why are you crying, Ted?" asked his Mom.

"Because my new sneakers hurt."

"That's because you put them on the wrong feet."

"But they're the only feet I have."

Ned: What does your Dad sell?

Ed: Salt.

Ned: Well, my dad is a salt seller, too.

Ed: Shake.

William: May I have some money for the man crying outside?
Mom: What crying man?
William: The one that's crying, "Ice cream! Ice cream!"

"Mom, can I please change my name right now?" asked Ben.. "But why would you want to do that, dear?" said his Mom. "Because Dad says he's going to spank me as sure as my name's Benjamin!"

Did you hear about the farmer's boy who hated the country?
He went to the big city and got a job as a shoeshine boy, and so the farmer made hay while the son shone!

The housewife answered a knock on the door and found a total stranger standing on the doorstep. "Excuse me for disturbing you, ma'am," he said politely, "but I pass your house every morning on my way to work, and I've noticed that every day you appear to be hitting your son on the head with a loaf of bread."

"That's right."

"Every day you wallop him on the head with a loaf of bread, and yet this morning you were hitting him with a chocolate cake . . .?"

"Well, today is his birthday."

An irate woman burst into the baker's shop and said, "I sent my son in for two pounds of cookies this morning, but when I weighed them there was only one pound. I suggest you check your scales." The baker looked at her calmly for a moment or two and then replied, "Ma'am, I suggest you weigh your son."

Was the carpenter's son a chip off the old block?

Doctor! Doctor! I think I'm going crazy. I have a carrot growing out of my ear.
Amazing! So you have. How could that have happened?
I can't understand it either, because I planted cabbage!

Dad: Why is your January report card so bad?
Son: Well, you know how it is. Things are always marked down after Christmas.

Why did Mr and Mrs Werewolf call their son Camera?
Because he was always snapping.

Will and Bill were quarrelling about whose father was the stronger. Will said, "Well, you know the Pacific Ocean? My father's the one who dug the hole for it."
Bill wasn't impressed, "Well, that's nothing. You know the Dead Sea? My father's the one who killed it."

Young Jimmy was having a snack after school with his Gran. "Would you like another cookie?" she asked.
"Yes, please," replied Jimmy.
"What good manners you have," said his Gran. "I do like to hear young people say 'please' and 'thank you'."
"I'll say them both if I can have a big piece of that cake," replied Jimmy.

A man whose son had just passed his driving test went home one evening and found that the boy had driven slap bang into the livingroom. "How did you manage to do that?" he fumed.

"Quite simple, Dad. I came in through the kitchen and turned left!"

"Your son is horribly spoiled," a concerned lady said to a proud mother one day. "How dare you!" she retorted, "my son's a perfect little gentleman."
"I'm afraid you haven't seen what the steamroller's done to him!"

He Said That Did He?

"Mom! There's a man at the door collecting for the Old Folks' Home. Shall I give him Grandma?"

When Dad came home he was astonished to see Alec sitting on a horse, writing something. "What on earth are you doing there?" he asked. "Well, the teacher told us to write an essay on our favorite animal. That's why I'm here and that's why Susie's sitting in the goldfish bowl!"

"Our teacher reminds me of the sea," said Alec to Billy.
"You mean she's deep, sometimes calm, but occasionally stormy?"
"No! She makes me sick."

My Uncle Ben and Aunt Flo haven't had a argument for five years.
That's wonderful!
Not really. Uncle Ben lives in China.

Miss Simons agreed to be interviewed by Alec for the school magazine. "How old are you Miss Simons?" asked Alec.

"I'm not going to tell you that."

"But Mr Hill the technical teacher and Mr Hill the geography teacher told me how old they were."

"Oh, well," said Miss Simon. "I'm the same age as both of them."

The poor teacher was not happy when she saw what Alec wrote: Miss Simons, our English teacher, confided in me that she was as old as the Hills.

Did you hear that Dumb Donald got splinters in his fingers? He'd been scratching his head!

A silly boy spent the afternoon with some friends, but when the time came for him to leave, a terrific storm started with thunder, lightning, and torrential rain. "You can't go home in this," said one of his friends, "you'd better stay the night."

"That's very kind of you," said the boy, "I'll just run home and get my pajamas."

Mommy, mommy, what's a werewolf?
Be quiet, John, and comb your face.

Mr Grouch was enraged when young Joe from next door began throwing stones at his greenhouse. "I'll teach you, you young rogue!" roared the furious neighbor. "I'll teach you to throw stones at my greenhouse!"
"I wish you would," said the insolent lad. "I've had three tries, and I haven't hit it yet!"

The swing doors of the Wild West saloon crashed open and in came Little Pete, black with fury.
"Alright!" he raged, "alright! Who did it? What goldarned varmint painted my horse blue?"
And the huge figure of Black Jake, notorious gunfighter and town baddie, rose from a chair by the door. "It were me, shrimp," he drawled, bunching his gigantic fists. "What about it?"
"Oh, well, er," stammered little Pete wretchedly, "all I wanted to say was . . . when are you going to give it another coat?"

"The girl beside me in math is very clever," said Alec to his mother. "She's got enough brains for two."

"Perhaps you'd better think of marriage," said Mom.

A certain little boy had been spanked by his father one morning. When his dad came in from the office that evening, the boy called out sulkily, "Mom! Your husband's just come home."

John kept pestering his parents to buy a video, but they said they couldn't afford one. So one day John came home clutching a package containing a brand-new video. "Where in the world did you get the money to pay for that?" asked his father suspiciously.
"It's OK, Dad," replied John, "I traded the TV in for it."

What did the dragon say when he saw St George in his shining armor?
Oh, no, not more tinned food!

Boy: Grandad, do you know how to croak?

Grandad: No, I don't think so. Why?

Boy: Because Daddy says he'll be a rich man when you do.

"I think my Dad is getting taller," said Stan to his friend.

"What makes you think that?"

"Well, lately I've noticed that his head is sticking through his hair."

Paddy and Mick were watching a John Wayne film on TV. In one scene John Wayne was riding madly towards a cliff. "I'll bet you $10 he falls over that cliff," said Paddy.
"Done," said Mick.
John Wayne rode straight over the cliff. As Mick handed over his $10, Paddy said, "I feel a bit guilty about this, I've seen the film before."
"So have I," said Mick, "but I didn't think he'd be stupid enough to make the same mistake twice."

Little Johnny and his mother were on a train. Johnny leant over and started to whisper in his mother's ear. "Johnny, how many times have I told you," said his mother, "it's rude to whisper. If you have something to say, say it out loud." "OK," said Johnny, "Why does the lady over there look like an ugly, haggard old witch?"

How do we know that Bob Geldoff is a wizard?
Because he started the Broomtown Rats.

Johnny collected lots of money from trick or treating and he went to the candy store to buy some chocolate. "You should give that money to charity," said the shopkeeper. Johnny thought for a moment and said, "No, I'll buy the chocolate. You give the money to charity."

"William, I've been told that you have been fighting with the boys next door," said Mom.
"Yes, but they're twins, so I wanted some way to tell them apart."

Uncle Hubert noticed that his nephew Johnny was watching him the whole time. "Why are you always looking at me?" he asked.
"I was just wondering when you were going to do your trick," replied Johnny.
"What trick?" enquired Uncle Hubert.
"Well, Mom and Dad say you drink like a fish."

One day Joe's mother turned to Joe's father and said, "It's such a nice day, I think I'll take Joe to the zoo."
"I wouldn't bother," said father. "If they want him, let them come and get him."

Eddie's father called up to him, "Eddie, if you don't stop playing that trumpet I think I'll go crazy!"
Eddy replied, "I think you are already, I stopped playing half an hour ago."

George knocked on the door of his friend's house. When his friend's mother answered he asked, "Can Albert come out to play?"
"No," said the mother, "it's too cold."
"Well, then," said George, "can his football come out to play?"

Charley: My cat likes to drink lemonade.
Farley: Golly, he sure must be a sourpuss.

Stan: Did you ever find your cat?
Dan: Yep, he was in the refrigerator.
Stan: Gosh, was he OK?
Dan: More than OK, he's a cool cat.

Ben's dad was building a pine bookshelf, and Ben was watching and occasionally helping. "What are the holes for?" Ben asked.
"They're knot holes," said his dad.
"What are they, then, if they're not holes?" asked Ben.

What's the difference between a Peeping Tom and someone who's just got out of the bath?
One is rude and nosey. The other is nude and rosey.

When Ben hit his thumb with a hammer he let out a few choice words. Shocked by her son's outburst, his mother said, "Don't you dare use that kind of language in this house."

"William Shakespeare did," replied Ben.

"Well, then, you'd better stop going around with him," said Mom.

Harry: Please may I have another pear, Miss Smith?

Teacher: Another, Harry? They don't grow on trees, you know.

Did you hear what Dumb Donald did when he offered to paint the garage for his dad in the summer vacation? The instructions said put on three coats, so he went in and put on his jacket, his raincoat and his overcoat.

Pa was taking Danny around the museum when they came across a magnificent stuffed lion in a glass case. "Pa," asked the puzzled Danny, "how did they shoot the lion without breaking the glass?"

Dick and Jane were arguing furiously over the breakfast table.

"Oh, you're so stupid!" shouted Dick.

"Dick!" said their father, "that's quite enough of that! Now say you're sorry."

"OK," said Dick. "Jane, I'm sorry you're stupid."

Mom: How can you practice your trumpet and listen to the radio at the same time?

Son: Easy. I have two ears.

Teddy came thundering down the stairs, much to his father's annoyance.

"Teddy," he called, "how many more times have I got to tell you to come down the stairs quietly? Now, go back up and come down like a civilized human being."

There was a silence, and Teddy reappeared in the front room.

"That's better," said his father. "Now, will you always come down stairs like that?"

"Suits me," said Teddy. "I slid down the bannister."

Miles: Our dog's just like one of the family.
Giles: Really? Which one?

Dan: I'm glad I'm not a bird.
Dad: Why?
Dan: Because I can't fly!

Jane: Do you ever do any gardening?
Wayne: Not often. Why?
Jane: You look as if you could do with some remedial weeding.

Jane: Have you noticed that your mother smells a bit funny these days?

Wayne: No. Why?

Jane: Well, your sister told me she was giving her a bottle of toilet water for her birthday.

Today, every Tom, Dick and Harry is called Wayne.

Harry was telling his friend about his holiday in Switzerland. His friend had never been to Switzerland, and asked, "What did you think of the scenery?"
"Oh, I couldn't see much," Harry admitted. "There were all these mountains in the way."

"Mom," yelled Johnny from the kitchen, "you know that dish you were always worried that I would break?"
"Yes, dear, what about it?"
"Well, your worries are over."

Tom: Why are you scratching your head?
Harry: I've got those arithmetic bugs again.
Tom: Arithmetic bugs – what are they?
Harry: Well, some people call them head lice.
Tom: Then why do you call them arithmetic bugs?
Harry: Because they add to my misery, subtract from my pleasure, divide my attention and multiply like crazy!

Who Needs Enemies?

Why do demons and ghouls get on so well?
Because demons are a ghoul's best friend.

What do you get if King Kong sits on your best friend?
A flat mate.

Where did Dr Jekyll find his best friend?
In Hyde Park.

John: I'm going to cross a galaxy with a frog.

Jim: You'd better not. You'll be sorry.

John: Why?

Jim: Don't you know what you'll get?

John: No. What?

Jim: Star warts.

Farley: Come on, Charley, I'll take you to the zoo.

Charley: If the zoo wants me, let them come and get me!

What did the termite say when he saw that his friends had completely eaten a chair?
"Wooden you know it!"

What did the croaking frog say to his friend?
"I think I've got a person in my throat."

What did the mouse say when his friend broke his front teeth?
"Hard cheese."

What did the owl say to his friend as he flew off?
"Owl be seeing you later."

What did the Loch Ness Monster say to his friend?
"Long time no sea."

Which of the witch's friends eats the fastest?
The goblin.

How does a witch make scrambled eggs?
She holds the pan and gets two friends to make the stove shake with fright.

Why does Dracula have no friends?
Because he's a pain in the neck!

Jed: If you eat any more ice cream, you'll burst.
Ned: OK. Pass the ice cream and duck.

What did the zombie's friend say when he introduced him to his girlfriend?
"Good grief! Where did you dig her up?"

Stan: I won 92 goldfish.
Fred: Where are you going to keep them?
Stan: In the bathroom.
Fred: But what will you do when you want to take a bath?
Stan: Blindfold them.

Ted said to his friend, "Can you lend me $10?"
"But I only have $8," his friend replied.
"That's OK, you can always owe me the other $2."

Did you hear about the wizard who turned his friend into an egg?
He kept trying to poach his ideas.

How does a skeleton call his friends?
On a telebone.

When a plane caught fire over the jungle the pilot ejected and landed in a cannibal's pot. The cannibal turned to his friend and said, "What's this flier doing in my soup?"

My friend is so stupid that he thinks twice before saying nothing.

After ice skating, two friends rushed home for a snack. "Will you join me in a cup of hot chocolate?" asked the first boy politely. "Sure," said his friend, "but do you think we'll both fit?"

A monster and a zombie went into the undertaker's. "I'd like to order a coffin for a friend of mine who has just died," said the monster. "Certainly, sir," said the undertaker, "but there was really no need to bring him with you."

Two aliens from outer space landed in Las Vegas and were wandering around the casinos. One of them volunteered to go inside and see what was happening. He came out looking rather shocked. "What's the matter?" asked his friend. "It's a very popular place," replied the first alien. "It's full of creatures that keep throwing up little metal disks."

Two monsters were working on building site. When lunchtime

came, one of them took out a box of sandwiches. "Rat paste and tomato," he moaned, as he bit into the first. "More rat paste and tomato," he muttered as he ate the second.

"Rat paste and tomato?" his friend asked as he picked up the third sandwich.

"Yes," sighed the monster. "I hate rat paste and tomato."

"Why don't you ask your wife to make you something different?"

The monster looked at him strangely. "I don't have a wife – I make my sandwiches myself."

My friend is so stupid he thinks that an autograph is a chart showing sales figures for cars.

The young teacher was complaining to his friends about how badly he was being paid. "We get a really poultry amount each month," he said.
"You mean 'paltry'," corrected one of his friends.
"No I don't, I mean 'poultry'," replied the teacher. "What I earn is chicken feed."

Two friends who lived in the town were chatting. "I've just bought a pig," said the first.
"But where will you keep it?" asked the second. "Your garden's much too small for a pig!"
"I'm going to keep it under my bed," replied his friend.
"But what about the smell?"
"He'll soon get used to that."

What should you call a polite, friendly, kind, good looking monster?
A failure.

Cannibal Boy: I've brought a friend home for dinner.
Cannibal Mom: Put him in the refrigerator and we'll have him tomorrow.

My friend is so silly that he spent two weeks in a revolving door looking for the doorknob!

Boy to Friend: I'm sorry, I won't be able to go out after school. I promised Dad that I would stay in and help him with my homework.

Why was the school principal not pleased when he bumped into an old friend?
They were both driving their cars at the time.

Boy to Friend: My dad is so old, when he was at school, history was called current events.

Mother to Friend: Johnny's so imaginative! I asked him what the "F" meant on his report, and he said "Fantastic."

Crossword fan: I've been trying to think of a word for two weeks!
Friend: How about a fortnight?

The big game hunter was showing his friends his hunting trophies. Drawing their attention to a lion-skin rug on the floor he said, "I shot this fellow in Africa. Didn't want to kill such a magnificent beast, of course, but it was either him or me."
"Well," said a guest, "he certainly makes a much better rug than you would!"

The proud owner of an impressive new clock was showing it off to a friend. "This clock," he said, "will go for 14 days without winding." "Really?" replied his friend. "And how long will it go if you do wind it?"

Knock, Knock

Knock, knock.
Who's there?
Tarzan.
Tarzan who?
Tarzan stripes forever!

Knock, knock.
Who's there?
Franz.
Franz who?
Franz, Romans, countrymen, lend me your ears!

Knock, knock.
Who's there?
Alec.
Alec who?
Alec most people but I don't like your face.

Knock, knock.
Who's there?
Iona.
Iona who?
Iona house of my own, you know.

Knock, knock.
Who's there?
Boo.
Boo who?
Please don't cry, it's only a joke!

Knock, knock.
Who's there?
Courtney.
Courtney who?
Courtney any robbers lately?

Knock, knock.
Who's there?
Arnold.
Arnold who?
Arnold boy who looks like a wizard.

Knock, knock.
Who's there?
Blood.
Blood who?
Blood brothers.

Knock, knock.
Who's there?
Owl.
Owl who?
Owl I can say is "knock, knock!"

Knock, knock.
Who's there?
Russia.
Russia who
Russia little bit faster or you'll be late.

Knock knock.
Who's there?
Harry.
Harry who?
Harry up! There's a ghost after us!

Knock knock.
Who's there?
Webster.
Webster who?
Webster Spin, your friendly
neighborhood spider.

Knock, knock.
Who's there?
Eye.
Eye who?
Eye know who you are!

Knock, knock.
Who's there?
Leg.
Leg who?
Leggo of me!

Knock, knock.
Who's there?
Iowa.
Iowa who?
Iowa lot to you.

Knock, knock.
Who's there?
Amos.
Amos who?
Amos quito.

Knock, knock.
Who's there?
Anna.
Anna who?
Anna 'nother mosquito.

Knock, knock.
Who's there?
Yetta.
Yetta who?
Yetta 'nother mosquito.

Knock, knock.
Who's there?
Helen.
Helen who?
Helen other mosquito!

Knock, knock.
Who's there?
Notta.
Notta who?
Notta 'nother mosquito!

Knock, knock.
Who's there?
Peas.
Peas who?
Peas to meet you.

Knock, knock.
Who's there?
Elly.
Elly who?
Ellymentary, my dear Watson!

Knock, knock.
Who's there?
Howl.
Howl who?
Howl I know when it's supper time?

Knock, knock.
Who's there?
Earl.
Earl who?
Earl tell you if you open the door.

Knock, knock.
Who's there?
Noah.
Noah who?
Noah don't know who you are either.

Knock, knock.
Who's there?
Ike.
Ike who?
Ike can see you through the keyhole!

Knock, knock.
Who's there?
Walter.
Walter who?
Walter, walter everywhere and not a drop to drink.

Knock, knock.
Who's there?
Doughnut.
Doughnut who?
Doughnut open the door, whatever you do!

Knock, knock.
Who's there?
Gorilla.
Gorilla who?
Gorilla hotdog, please.

Knock, knock.
Who's there?
Cereal.
Cereal who?
Cereal pleasure to have met you.

Knock, knock.
Who's there?
Dismay.
Dismay who?
Dismay surprize you but I'm from New York.

Knock, knock.
Who's there?
Heywood.
Heywood who?
Heywood you open the door?

Knock, knock.
Who's there?
Euripides.
Euripides who?
Euripides pants, you menda deez pants.

Knock, knock.
Who's there?
Gopher.
Gopher who?
Gopher help, I'm stuck in the elevator!

Knock, knock.
Who's there?
Muffin.
Muffin who?
Muffin to declare.

Knock, knock.
Who's there?
Oil.
Oil who?
Oil be seeing you.

Knock, knock.
Who's there?
Dutch.
Dutch who?
Dutch my hands – they're freezing!

Knock, knock.
Who's there?
Money.
Money who?
Money is hurt, I knocked it playing football.

Knock, knock.
Who's there?
Lionel.
Lionel who?
Lionel roar if you step on its tail.

Graffiti Rules, OK

Homer wrote The Oddity.

Tolkien is hobbit-forming.

Yorik is a numb-skull.

If you cross an elephant with a goldfish, would you get swimming trunks?

Alas, poor Kilroy, I knew him backwards.

Cowardice rules, if that's alright with the rest of you.

Never hit a man when he's down. He might get up again.

Happiness can't buy money.

Subways are always in a hole.

Pedestrians must walk.

Isaac Newton counts on his fingers.

Don't lose any sleep over insomnia.

Amnesia rules. O . . .

Today's pigs are tomorrow's bacon.

Why does Christmas always come when the shops are so busy?

Latin is the language of the dead.

Everybody hates graffitiists. I hate everyone – graffitiists.

Keep the US tidy, post your garbage abroad.

Do unto others before they have a chance to do it unto you.

Don't get angry, get even.

Stop a head cold going to your chest, tie a knot in your neck.

Modern music isn't as bad as it sounds.

I can't remember if I used to be forgetful or not.

The best way to talk to a lion is by long distance telephone. Sorry, lion's busy.

Moses found in a basket – reed all about it.

Preserve wildlife – pickle a hedgehog today!

Be alert – your country needs lerts.

Remember: when eating an elephant, take one bite at a time.

Nostalgia rules, hokey cokey.

Shoplifters have the gift of the grab.

I came to the zoo when I was seven, which cage were you in?

Once there was an elephant who went away to forget.

Elephants are modest – they bathe with their trunks.

Modesty is wearing swimming trunks with sleeves.

Why is water wet?

Why is there air?

Is there intelligent life on Earth? Yes, but I'm only visiting.

Act your age, not your shoe size.

Communicate with a fish – drop it a line.

Between your eyes is something that smells.

Telepathy is a code invented by Morse.

Apathy rules, so what?

Wood doesn't grow on trees you know!

Save trees – eat a beaver.

Do you have trouble making up your mind? Well, yes and no.

I'd give my right hand to be ambidextrous.

Do Vikings use Norse code?

James Bond rules, OOK.

Dyslexia rules, K.O.

Escalators are on the way up.

Breakfast in London, lunch in New York, baggage in Bermuda.

Can you help me out? Which way did you come in?

Exits are on the way out.

I don't care whether I win or lose, as long as I win.

I think, therefore I am.
I am, therefore I think.
I'm pink, therefore I'm Spam.

Mickey Mouse is a rat.

Watership Down: you've read the book, you've seen the film, now try the stew.

Dracula is a pain the the neck.

Dracula loves in vein.

I used to be a werewolf but I'm OK nowooooooooh.

Have you seen the invisible man lately?

This wall is available in paperback.

Who was Corporal Punishment?

I've lived on Earth all my life.

Why do trains leave tracks behind them?

Stop, look, and listen and be hit by a train.

If Superman is so clever, why does he wear his underpants outside his trousers?

If God had meant us to fly, he would have given us wings or sent us the tickets.

He who laughs last doesn't get the joke.

And the meek shall inherit the earth, as long as nobody minds.

Don't play in the street – you may get that run down feeling.

Poetry is when every line starts with a capital letter.

Handel was a boy in a story by Grimm. He had a sister called Gristle.

Saint Peter was a rabbit in a book by Beatrix Potter.

The Housing Problem by Rufus Quick.

In the Country by Theresa Green.

Shakespeare wrote tragedy, comedy and errors.

If all the world's a stage and all the men and women merely players, where does the audience come from?

The Venus de Milo is perfectly armless.

If you cannot spell a word, look it up in a dikshunary.

The Pope lives in the Vacuum.

The only good book's a read one.

Sing and shout and dance with joy
For I was here before Kilroy.

Praktiss maikes purfikt.

If you cannot communicate, try talking.

Monkey is the root to all people.

My needlework teacher is a sew-in-sew.

When volkswagens retire, do they go to the old volks home?

Ridiculous Riddles

What does a garden say when it laughs?
Hoe, hoe, hoe.

Why is a garden like a story?
Because they both have plots.

What is it that's given to you, but is used more by other people?
Your name.

Why did the jelly roll?
Because it saw the apple turnover.

Why would a sixth sense be a handicap?
Because it would be a new sense.

What animal keeps the best time?
A watchdog.

What is found in the middle of both America and Australia?
The letter "R".

Why is mayonnaise never ready?
Because it's always dressing.

Why did the cat stare at the garage light?
He was trying to make a moth bawl.

What is round and has a terrible temper?
A vicious circle.

Why were the elephants the last animals off the ark?
They had to pack their trunks.

How do you make notes of stone?
Rearrange the letters!

Which Congressman wears the biggest hat?
The one with the largest head.

When is a door not a door?
When it's ajar.

When is a car not a car?
When it turns into a garage.

How do elephants climb trees?
They sit on an acorn and wait for it to grow.

How do elephants climb down from trees?
They sit on a leaf and wait til fall.

How many elephants can you get into a small car?
Four: two in the front and two in the back.

How many rhinoceroses can you get into a small car?
None, it's full of elephants.

What do you call a shrimp with a machine gun?
Al Caprawn.

What lives at the bottom of the sea and shakes?
A nervous wreck.

What's harder to catch the faster you run?
Your breath.

What's black and white and red all over?
A newspaper.

What has a neck but no head?
A bottle.

When are eyes not eyes?
When the wind makes them water.

What can speak every language but has never been to school?
An echo.

What is the biggest ant?
An elephant.

What is gray and has a trunk?
A mouse going on vacation.

What does a baby ape sleep in?
An apricot.

What amount of money can be divided fifty-fifty between two people giving one of them a hundred times more than the other?
Fifty dollars and fifty cents.

When will a net hold water?
When the water has turned to ice.

What's the difference between a running man and a running dog?
One wears trousers, and the other pants.

What letter is nine inches long?
The letter "Y": it's one quarter of a yard.

What dish is out of this world?
A flying saucer.

What is the shortest month?
May. It has only three letters.

What branch of the military do babies join?
The infantry.

Why do you go to bed?
Because the bed won't come to you.

What's in the church, but not the steeple,
The minister has it, but not the people?
The letter "R."

What is the difference between a cat and a match?
One lights on its feet, the other lights on its head.

What goes 99 thump, 99 thump?
A centipede with a wooden leg.

How can you tell if there are
elephants in your refrigerator?
Footprints in the cream cheese.

What is the difference between a dog and a flea?
A dog can have fleas, but flea can't have dogs.

What's the difference between a hungry man and a greedy man?
One longs to eat and the other eats too long.

What's the difference between a thief and a church bell?
One steals from the people, the other peals from the steeple.

What's the difference between a beached vessel and a wrecked airplane?
One grounds on the land and the other lands on the ground.

What is the difference between an oak tree and a tight shoe?
One makes acorns, the other corns ache.

Why did the spy pull the sheets over his head?
He was an undercover agent.

What's the difference between the business of a removal firm and a shop that sells note paper?
One's moving, the other's stationery.

Why did the boy take a bicycle to bed?
Because he didn't want to walk in his sleep.

What should you always keep because no one else wants it?
Your temper.

Why couldn't the mountain climber call for help?
Because he was hanging by his teeth.

Why is an empty purse always the same?
Because there's never any change in it.

What part of a clock is always old?
The second hand.

What are two things you can never have for breakfast?
Lunch and dinner.

Why did the computer get arrested?
Because it was robbing the memory bank.

Why did the boy wear a wet shirt all day?
Because the label said "wash and wear."

What sound does a whale make when it cries?
Blubber, blubber, blubber.

Why do cows wear bells?
Because their horns won't work.

What kind of paper makes the best paper airplanes?
Fly paper.

What do you call a foreign ant?
An important.

If your watch is broken, why can't you go fishing?
Because you haven't the time.

How can you make a slow horse fast?
Don't give him any food.

What kind of animal needs oil?
A mouse – it squeaks!

What is dark but made by light?
A shadow.

Why is a piano like an eye?
Because they are both closed when their lids are down.

What can be right but never wrong?
An angle.

What is full of holes but holds water?
A sponge.

What is green and can jump a mile a minute?
A grasshopper with hiccups!

Why did the gardener throw roses into the burning building?
He heard that flowers grew better in hothouses.

What did the big chimney say to the little chinmey?
"You're too young to smoke!"

What is a dimple?
A pimple going the other way.

Which eye gets hit the most?
The bulls-eye.

Why was the dog chasing his tail?
He was trying to make both ends meet.

What sort of band doesn't make music?
A rubber band.

What is the difference between an old man and a cow?
One lives in the past, the other in the pasture.

What is the best way to win a race?
Run faster than anyone else!

What happened when the boy sat on a pin?
Nothing – it was a safety pin.

Why did Moses lose the race?
Because the Lord told him to come forth.

Who drives away all his customers?
A taxi-driver.

What sick bird is unlawful?
An ill-eagle.

Why is 4,840 square yards like a bad tooth?
Because it is an acre.

Is it dangerous to swim on a full stomach?
Yes, it is better to swim in the water!

Why is a shoemaker like a minister?
Because they both try to save soles (souls).

What would you call two banana skins?
A pair of slippers.

What's the best thing to make in a hurry?
Haste.

If two wrongs don't make a right, what did two rights make?
An airplane.

Where does a two-ton gorilla sleep?
Anywhere he wants to.

If you found a five dollar bill in every pocket of your coat, what would you have?
Someone else's coat.

When do two and two make more than four.
When they make 22.

What is the latest thing in dresses?
A nightdress.

What increases its value by being turned upside down?
The number 6.

What is the best way to hunt bear?
With your clothes off!

Why is a lame dog like a boy adding six and seven?
Because he puts down three and carries one.

What is a doughnut?
A person who is crazy about money.

Why can two very thin people not become good friends?
They must always be slight acquaintances.

What did the quarter say when it got stuck in the slot?
Money's tight these days.

Why is snow different from Sunday?

Because it can fall on any day of the week.

There Once Was a Bad Guy . . .

There once was a kid named
Darren
Whose room was surprisingly
barren.
He had no toys
Like all normal boys,
But he did believe in sharing

A cannibal known as Ned
Ate potato chips in his bed.
His mother said, "Sonny,
It's not very funny.
Why don't you eat people instead?"

There once was a writer named Wright
Who instructed his son to write right.
He said, "Son, write Wright right.
It's not right to write Wright
as 'rite' – try to write Wright all right!"

There once was a consumer named Phil
Who really wanted to kill
A sly young vendor
Who made him a big spender
And gave him a very large bill.

There once was a boy from Brazil
Who of pumpkin ate more than his
fill.
He thought it no matter,
That he grew fatter and fatter,
But he burst – which makes me
quite ill.

There once was a guy named Matt
Who had an overly large cat.
When it chased a mouse
It shook the whole house
So Matt got rid of the cat.

There was an old man of Philly
Who was hooked on the movie
"Free Willy."
He quit his job at the jail,
for a dolphin and whale,
And so was the life of Wee Willy.

There was an young fellow called
Jake
Who had a poisonous snake.
It bit his head
And now he's dead
So that was the end of Jake.

There once was a boy from
Montreal
Who loved to play basketball.
For a team he tried out
But if he made it, I doubt
For you see, he was three feet tall!

There was a young man named
Wyatt
whose voice was exceedingly
quiet,
And then one day
it faded away.

There was a young hunter named
Shepherd
Who was eaten for lunch by a
leopard.
Said the leopard, "Egad!
You'd be tastier, lad,
If you had been salted and
peppered!"

A junior school dropout named Ray
Once had an unusual day.
Entrusting his fate
To a twenty-pound weight,
While a hurricane blew him away.

An unlucky fellow named Foster
Caught a mermaid while fishing
off Gloucester.
To his lasting regret,
When he reached in the net,
She slipped through his hands
and he lost her.

There was a young man from
Quebec
Who wrapped both his legs round
his neck!
But then he forgot
How to undo the knot,
And now he's an absolute wreck!

There was a young man called Art,
Who thought he'd be terribly
smart.
He ate ten cans of beans,
And busted his jeans,
With a loud and earth-shattering
****!

While visiting close friends, a gnat,
Decided to sleep in a hat.
But an elderly guest
Decided to rest,
Now the gnat and the hat are
quite flat.

A blackberry picker called Sam
Ate berries where others ate ham.
A doctor, who pried,
Said, "Sir, your inside
Would make most delectable jam."

There was a young lad of St Just
Who ate apple pie till he bust.
It wasn't the fru-it
That caused him to do it,
What finished him off was the crust.

Said a very l-o-n-g crocodile,
"My length is a terrible trial!
I know I should diet
but each time I try it
I'm hungry for more than a mile!"
(Lilian Moore)

I don't wish to harp about Lew
Who kept peering into the stew.
He lifted the lid
And in it he slid
I think I'll miss dinner, don't you?

There was an old man of
Thermopylae,
Who never did anything properly;
But they said, "If you choose,
To boil eggs in your shoes,
You shall never remain in
Thermopylae.
(Edward Lear)

There was a young parson named
Perkins
Exceedingly fond of small
gherkins.
One summer at tea
He ate forty-three,
Which pickled his internal workin's.

Our kitten, the one we call Louie,
Will never eat liver so chewy.
Nor the milk, nor the fish
that we put in his dish.
He only will dine on chop suey.

There was a young boy of Quebec
Who fell into the ice to his neck.
When asked, "Are you friz?"
He replied, "Yes, I is,
But we don't call this cold in
Quebec."

A whale liked to eat portions
double.
Nothing he ate gave him trouble.
But he just couldn't cope
With two bars of soap,
And he now blows a whale of a
bubble.
(Lilian Moore)

There was an old man in a barge
Whose nose was exceedingly
large;
But in fishing by night,
It supported a light,
Which helped that old man in a
barge.
(Edward Lear)

There was an old baker of Rye
Who was baked by mistake in a pie.
To the household's disgust
He emerged through the crust,
And exclaimed, with a yawn,
"Where am I?"

Get Your Mouth Around These!

Peter Piper picked a peck of pickled peppers.
If Peter Piper picked a peck of pickled peppers, how many peppers did Peter Piper pick?

What noise annoys an oyster?
A noisy noise annoys an oyster most.

"Night, night, Knight," said one knight to the other knight.
"Night, night, Knight."

Nine nimble noblemen nibble nuts.

Our Joe wants to know if your Joe will lend our Joe your Joe's banjo. If your Joe won't lend our Joe your Joe's banjo, our Joe won't lend your Joe our Joe's banjo when our Joe has a banjo!

The gleaming glass glowed on the grass.

The frozen fishermen threw their fish back in again.

Sam Slick sawed six slimy, slippery side saplings.

The flyer furled the flaring flag and flung it firmly from the fuselage.

If a dog chews shoes what shoes should he choose to chew?

Tommy Turner turned away from moral turpitude and tried to teach the two virtues of tolerance and tranquility to his twins.

Mrs Lister's sister spoke Spanish, Swedish and Swahili and spent a season in the Sudan where she suffered from sunstroke.

Timothy Tiddles twiddled tightly twisted twine ten times to test it.

Quixotic topic.

A laurel-crowned clown.

He ran from the Indies to the Andes in his undies.

Chimes challenged the changing year.

Yellow butter, purple jelly, red jam, black bread.

Is there a pleasant peasant
present?

If Roland Reynolds rolled a round
roll
Round a round room,
Where is the round roll which
Roland Reynolds rolled
Round the room?

How much wood would a
woodchuck chuck,
If a woodchuck could chuck wood?

Many Mau-Mau meandered among the marshes, looking for the missing missionary.

The wild wind whipped Walt from the wharf.

The architect was extraordinarily efficient and effective and excitedly explored the excavations evincing exaggerated exuberance.

Once upon a barren moor
There dwelt a bear, also a boar.
The bear could not bear the boar,
The boar thought the bear a bore.
At last the bear could bear no more
That boar that bored him on the moor.
And so one morn he bored the boar –
That boar will bore the bear no more!

If a shipshape ship shop stocks six shipshape shop-soiled ships,
How many shipshape shop-soiled ships would six shipshape ship shops stock?

One hundred air-inhaling elephants.

Dashing Daniel defied David to deliver Dora from the dawning danger.

United States twin-screw steel cruisers.

Eight gray geese gazing gaily into Greece.

Red leather,
Yellow leather!

A big blue bucket of blue blueberries.

A twister of twists
Once twisted a twist,
And the twist that he twisted
Was a three-twisted twist.
Now in twisting this twist,
If a twist should untwist,
The twist that untwisted
Would untwist the twist.

She sells sea shells by the sea shore.

Thin sticks,
Thick bricks.

Round and round the rugged rocks the ragged rascal ran.

Bobby beat a bit of butter to make a better batter.

Old Dunn,
Young dunn,
And Old Dunn's son.

Young Dunn,
Will be Dunn,
When Old Dunn's done.

Tommy Tye
Tried to tie his tie,
But tugging too tight
Tore his tie.
Tom turned to Ted.
Told Ted to try
To tie the tie
Tom tried to tie.

Rupert wrestled rashly with Robin.

Clearly the clause in Claus's
contract causes Claus confusion.

The sloth loafs among the low slopes.

Rubber baby-buggy bumpers.